Teaching grammar comm

Other titles in the NETWORD series

NETWORD 1 — A toolkit for talking: strategies for independent communication
by Duncan Sidwell
Discusses classroom conditions and teaching techniques which will encourage students to progress to independent use of the foreign language. Principles of methodology are supported by many examples of information gap and graded activities.
240 x 210mm, paperback, 72 pages, ISBN 1 874016 17 8, £7.50

NETWORD 2 — Language games and activities
by John Langran and Sue Purcell
Each of thirteen games in the book is described in detail, with full instructions for exploitation, and is given as an example of a principle or strategy which can be re-used with a different language, at different levels, with different groups and for different purposes.
240 x 210mm, paperback, 64 pages, ISBN 1 874016 23 2, £7.50

NETWORD 3 — Mixed-ability teaching: meeting learners' needs
by Susan Ainslie
Offers strategies for differentiation between individual learners in a group, which will help the learner to achieve his or her learning potential. A range of suggested practical activities will be useful for individual tutors or as a basis for group work.
240 x 210mm, paperback, 60 pages, ISBN 1 874016 33 X, £7.50

NETWORD 4 — Assessing adult learners
by Susan Ainslie and Alwena Lamping
This book looks at ways of integrating assessment into the teaching programme. It offers practical suggestions on creating and choosing appropriate assessment materials, collecting evidence of competence, assessment techniques and managing assessment in the classroom. The final chapter considers formal accreditation and provides guidelines on how to choose from the range of accreditation on offer in the UK.
240 x 210mm, paperback, 68 pages, ISBN 1 874016 39 9, £7.50

NETWORD 5 — Maintaining motivation: strategies for improving retention rates in adult education language classes
by Alwena Lamping and Christine Ball
The aim of this book is to contribute to the discussion on how to prevent learners dropping out in the first place by: exploring the reasons why learners leave a course; considering how to sustain their initial motivation; proposing tried and tested strategies to employ at various key times; providing a range of ideas for practical activities; offering a series of 'troubleshooting' measures to cope with problems and encourage learners to stay the course.
240 x 210mm, paperback, 78 pages, ISBN 1 874016 68 2, £8.00

CILT publications are available through all good booksellers and from the national network of Comenius Centres, Scottish CILT, and Northern Ireland CILT (further details on 0171 379 5101). Orders may also be sent to CILT's distributor: Grantham Book Services Ltd, Isaac Newton Way, Alma Park Industrial Estate, Grantham, Lincs NG31 9SD. Telephone credit card orders to: 01476 541 080, fax orders to 01476 541 061.

Visitors to the Information and Resources Library at CILT, 20 Bedfordbury, London, WC2N 4LB (telephone 0171 379 5110) receive a 10% discount on all CILT publications, CILT Direct subscribers receive a 15% discount.

NETWORD 6

TEACHING LANGUAGES TO ADULTS

Teaching grammar communicatively

Sue Purcell

Cartoons by Joanne Bond

The views expressed in this publication are the author's and do not necessarily represent those of CILT.

Acknowledgements

Ute Hitchin of CILT for her help and constructive advice during the writing of this book. Also my colleagues within Surrey Adult Education Service who are always willing to share ideas. Not least my students and former students who have acted as guinea pigs for the ideas in this book.

First published 1997
© 1997 Centre for Information on Language Teaching and Research
ISBN 1 874016 91 7

Cover by Neil Alexander
Printed in Great Britain by Copyprint UK Ltd

Published by the Centre for Information on Language Teaching and Research, 20 Bedfordbury, Covent Garden, London WC2N 4LB.

Only the worksheets and role-cards may be photocopied by teachers for classroom use. Apart from this, no part of this publication may be reproduced, stored in a retrieval system, or transmitted in any form or by any means, electronic, mechanical, photocopying, recording, or otherwise, without the prior permission of the Copyright owner.

Contents

			Page
Introduction			1
Chapter 1	**What is communicative grammar teaching?**		4
	Relevance to learners' needs		5
	Meaningful and purposeful language		5
	Authenticity and unpredictability		6
	Personalisation		6
	Over to you		7
Chapter 2	**A way in**		8
	Encourage grammatical awareness among learners		8
	Over to you		10
	Allow learners to discover rules for themselves		10
	Only teach what learners need to know now		12
	How much grammatical terminology to use		14
	Treat correction of errors as part of the learning process		15
	Over to you		18
Chapter 3	**Techniques**		19
	Take one thing at a time		19
	Relate the new to the known		21
	Expose learners to unknown grammar in natural situations		22
	Illustrate and demonstrate, don't explain		23
	Make it fun		26
	Surveys		29
	Over to you		29

Chapter 4	**Examples of presentation of grammar points**	30
	Simple past tense in English	30
	Over to you	35
	Word order in subordinate clauses in German	35
	Over to you	37
	Direct object pronouns in French	37
	Over to you	41
	Possessive adjectives in German	41
	Over to you	46
	The use of the genitive case after the negative in Russian	46
	Over to you	49
	Comparative of adjectives in English	49
	Over to you	52

Conclusion 53

Further reading and resources 54

Introduction

Why teach grammar?

If a foreigner says to me in broken English 'me want you go restaurant tonight', then I can understand perfectly. The foreigner does not have to use the correct grammar for me to realise that he or she is inviting me to dinner; the words used are sufficient to communicate the message. Should I decide to go out to dinner with this person, however, I know that I do not exactly have an evening's scintillating conversation to look forward to; I know that I will have to talk slowly, using simple structures and that we will certainly not get around to discussing opinions and emotions. We will be communicating at a very basic level.

This level of communication may well be a worthwhile goal in itself for some language learners. People who travel all over the world on business may find it more useful for their purposes to have a smattering of several languages than to concentrate on learning the grammar of one language and floundering in the other countries they visit. If I were to book, at short notice, a once-in-a-lifetime holiday to Rio, memorising a few set phrases and learning some basic vocabulary would be of more practical benefit to me than were I to spend the same amount of time and effort on learning Portuguese grammatical structures.

On the other hand, there are situations when such a basic level of communication is not appropriate. Would we be happy with our immigration officers saying 'visa no good, go away!' instead of 'I'm sorry, your papers are not in order and I cannot allow you to enter Britain'? Would our business people be taken seriously in their negotiations if they asked for a discount by saying 'me want it more cheap'?

If we want to be taken seriously and treated as an equal in another country, we need to speak accurately, which means having an understanding of the grammatical structure of that language. We may be able to get away without grammar if we only intend to order a few drinks and buy stamps and postcards on holiday, but if we intend to live, work or study in another country, if we want to converse with friends or our children's in-laws or if we want to pass an examination, then we need more than just vocabulary — we need grammar.

'Me want you go restaurant tonight' will be understood by most native English speakers despite its grammatical inaccuracy, but a poor grasp of the grammatical rules relating to endings, tenses and so on **can** cause misunderstanding sometimes leading to confusion, embarrassment or even an outbreak of general hilarity among native speakers of the foreign language with **you** as the butt of the joke.

One of my own students completely flummoxed a Moscow post office clerk by her request for ten carrots; she had put a masculine ending -*ov* on a feminine noun *marka*, ending up with the word *markov*, the Russian for carrots.

An English learner might say '*Ich habe vor zehn Jahren in Dorking gewohnt*' (I lived in Dorking ten years ago); perfect grammar, you might think, but you will have got completely the wrong idea if what the speaker actually meant was 'I have been living in Dorking for ten years' (*ich wohne seit zehn Jahren in Dorking*).

Without a knowledge of Russian case endings you may be embarrassed to find out that the name Borisova in a text or conversation could refer to Mr Borisov, in the accusative or genitive case, as opposed to Mrs Borisova in the nominative.

It is very difficult to 'unlearn' bad habits, as they become deeply entrenched. If, when learners begin a foreign language, they are told that gender doesn't matter and are never corrected, getting away with *le gare* one week, *la gare* the next, they will find eradicating errors very difficult later, should they develop a greater interest in the language and start taking it more seriously. We know we are making a mistake in our own language when something does not sound right. Ideally, learners should strive to reach the same situation in another language, but if they have never been taught to distinguish the correct version from the incorrect in the first place, they will never reach that stage. It is just as easy to learn *das Geld* as *der Geld*, so why not teach learners the correct version right from the start?

It is possible to learn whole phrases and sentences parrot fashion — in fact, learners could probably pass lower level examinations without a deep understanding of a language's structure — but they cannot go on piling more and more set phrases into their head and memorising them. If they are taught to recognise patterns and models in a language, then they only have to learn one model in order to be able to substitute various vocabulary within it. If, in the early days of learning German, students master the correct accusative ending *'Gibt es in der Nähe **einen** Supermarkt?'* then it is easy enough to substitute any word to suit their needs later on, e.g. *'Gibt es einen Sonderrabatt?'*

Rules, once learnt, can be correctly applied in an infinite number of utterances. When learners can control and manipulate language to suit their needs, they will have reached the stage of complete autonomy. Then, armed only with a dictionary, they will have the freedom to choose whatever they want to say and to whom.

What is communicative grammar teaching?

Chapter 1

Many tutors are confused as to whether they should teach grammar at all. Instead of the existence of consensus and definitive guidelines, myths and rumours abound such as 'grammar is boring', 'grammar is difficult', 'teaching grammar is old-fashioned'.

It is true that there has been a backlash against the grammar-translation method of teaching foreign languages so popular thirty years ago. The grammar-translation method concentrated on the written language; grammatical rules were emphasised and a wrong ending — *den* instead of *dem,* for instance — would be frowned upon. Teachers themselves would rarely use the target language in class, and what oral work there was tended to consist of drills, artificially constructed to practise a specific grammatical point. The result was that learners knew a lot **about** the language, but were not capable of **using** it to talk to people.

There then followed a complete sea-change in the thinking behind teaching languages. The key word was communication; the message was more important than how you said it. Success in learning a foreign language was measured by whether you would be understood by that mythical paragon — the sympathetic native speaker. As a result, the importance of accuracy was downgraded.

As has already been mentioned, inaccuracy **does** have a negative effect on communication, and the way you speak colours other people's perceptions of you. These factors are now being recognised and the pendulum has swung back again, although certainly not all the way.

Today, we talk about the 'communicative approach' to language teaching. This is not a hard and fast theory but is an amalgam of different principles prevalent at one time or other in the past. The communicative approach recognises that the primary purpose of language is communication, but it also accepts that human beings are able to use their brains cognitively and can thus be trained to recognise patterns and transfer and apply rules to other situations, not only those they have heard and practised in class.

What are the key features of a communicative approach?

The communicative approach takes the learners' needs as its starting point and says 'what do people need to know if they travel to the target country or meet a native speaker? Okay, I'll teach that first'.

Relevance to learners' needs

So, in Russian, you would teach numbers early on in a course to help people cope with shopping and prices, even though they are a notoriously difficult topic. You would, of course, not go into the declensions of numbers nor the full range of endings they govern. Beginners do not need to be taught rules for forming the imperative, but phrases like 'excuse me', 'tell me' and 'show me' will be taught quite early on in the course when using a communicative approach. Learners will find the question '*Comment vous appelez-vous?*' very useful right from the early stages of learning, but they can use it without having to know all the rules on word order with reflexive verbs.

In real life we use language to find out something we do not know. If you and I were both sitting looking at a clock, I would not ask you 'What time is it?' I can see the time, so why on earth do I need to ask? In a language class this sort of activity is used merely to practise the structure, but the language is not being used in a meaningful way, i.e. for a genuine reason. If, however, I could not see the clock because it was turned away from me but I wanted to know the time, I would have to ask 'What time is it?' I am saying exactly the same thing, but this time there is a purpose to my asking the question.

Meaningful and purposeful language

Most of the language taught in an adult course can be presented and practised in meaningful ways. It just requires a little bit of forethought from tutors in thinking up realistic contexts and situations. Times can be extensively practised within the context of the information bureau in a railway station, with some learners (or the tutor) having access to a timetable and others having to ask about train departures and arrivals or plan an itinerary. Similarly, a diary exercise, where learners have to negotiate a suitable time to meet, will contain lots of practice of time expressions.

Authenticity and unpredictability

Traditional grammar drills and contrived dialogues are usually so tedious and monotonous because they use artificial, carefully limited language and follow a predictable pattern. Learners know what is coming next and can generally produce the correct form without necessarily understanding a word.

Real speakers of foreign languages do not behave predictably. If I ask someone the time, they might say 'It is half past two', but they are just as likely to say 'It's half two' or 'It's two thirty'. They might even say 'Pardon?', 'I'm sorry, I haven't got a watch' or 'I'm not sure, I think I'm fast'. We cannot be sure how our learners' questions will be answered in the target country, but we can give them plenty of exposure to a range of options, including the unexpected, and we can train them to **listen** to the answer instead of expecting a standard response.

Nowadays textbooks use authentic materials for reading practice and authentic dialogues recorded naturally in and around the target country. The language may not even be perfect, there will be hesitations, repetition, some grammatical errors but it will be spoken by real native speakers in natural situations. This might be harder for learners at the time, who would prefer to listen to dialogues recorded in sound-proof studios by professional actors speaking slowly and clearly, but it will be of more benefit in the long run when they have to cope with 'real' speech.

Personalisation

When everyday conversations are analysed, it is noted that people use the pronouns 'I' and 'you' far more than the other parts of the verb. The communicative classroom will therefore encourage learners to talk about themselves, their own needs, likes and dislikes and so on and ask for the same information from others, perhaps even conduct a survey of others' views.

The traditional grammatical approach used a disproportionate amount of language in the third person; for example, questions on a picture story would include 'What is the man doing?', 'Where does she go next?', etc. There is nothing wrong with using a picture story, but it can easily be turned into a more personalised, hence communicative exercise by the tutor giving the instructions 'Imagine you are the man in this story, tell me what happened to you last week'. The forms practised will prove to be much more useful in real conversations later.

1. What is communicative grammar teaching?

Tutors have always taught the present tense, the accusative case, the passive voice and so on. What has changed is the way these topics are taught. Often only very minor changes are needed to turn a dry grammar lesson into a meaningful, relevant and enjoyable one.

Over to you

How communicative is your current approach to teaching? Which of the following do you use in your classes?

1	Activities and contexts which are relevant to the learners' needs. If you are teaching a language for business purposes, are the tasks you set and the vocabulary you teach relevant, or are they more appropriate for people visiting the country as tourists?
2	Language used in a meaningful and realistic way. Do you use information gap activities? Is there a purpose to using the target language or is it used artificially merely to practise a particular structure?
3	Authentic listening and reading material. Do you have a collection of menus, timetables, bus tickets, advertisements, etc that you have gathered, sitting unused in a box? Could you devise role plays using them?
4	Personalised tasks. Do learners use mostly the first and second persons of the verb when they speak the target language? Devise a survey or questionnaire to encourage learners to talk about themselves. How many grammatical structures could be practised using the simple technique of 'find someone who . . .?'

A way in

Chapter 2

Encourage grammatical awareness among learners

Many native English speakers are unaware of the grammar in their own and other languages. Children in British schools do not, on the whole, have lessons dedicated to grammar. Since English is a language with few ending changes and just one definite article 'the', native English speakers often find the role that grammar plays in other languages difficult to comprehend.

The importance of grammar can be stressed implicitly right from the early lessons of a course. Each time you write new vocabulary on the board, write up the appropriate article along with nouns and insist learners do so in their own notebooks. Advise them to learn and say the correct gender along with the noun right from the start. Do not write grammatical structures on the board out of context. Just writing up *otros, Herrn Schmidt* or *je parte* is meaningless and when learners come to review their notes at a later date, they will not remember the significance of those forms. Write up a whole phrase which exemplifies **why** that particular form is used, e.g. *en otros colores, mit Herrn Schmidt* and *il faut que je parte*.

Anticipate what difficulties English speaking learners may have in the foreign language. Past tenses, e.g. *j'ai fait, he hecho,* often cause few problems, since learners relate them to similar patterns in English such as 'I have done'. The use of the present tense with *depuis* and *seit,* on the other hand, frequently does prove difficult for English learners to master because we use a different tense in English.

Every year I know that several people in my beginners' Russian class will not see why the word for Moscow is different in the two sentences 'I am going to Moscow' and 'He studies at Moscow University', because they are unable to distinguish between a noun and an adjective. Similarly, many learners will not see why a different word for 'what' is used in the sentences 'What colour is it?' and 'What is it?' The word 'before' frequently causes problems; is it a preposition as in 'before the lesson', a conjunction as in 'before the lesson started' or an adverb as in 'before, the lesson was held in the language laboratory'? How to translate 'when' often foxes students of German; should it be *wann, wenn* or *als*?

Knowing what structures are likely to be misunderstood or difficult to grasp means that you can take more time when presenting them, pointing out other clues in the sentence that will help learners choose the correct word; *als*, for example, will be accompanied by a verb in the past tense. It is trying to translate literally from English, where one word can fulfil a broad range of functions, which is usually responsible for coming out with the wrong word. Keep on reminding learners that they cannot do this.

When you set your class a listening comprehension task, learners usually concentrate on listening for meaning; they rarely pay attention to the form of the language being used. This means that in a sentence like '*J'aime le poisson, la soupe, le fromage et les fruits, mais je n'aime pas la viande*' students will be listening to the nouns, particularly if the comprehension question was 'What are the speaker's likes and dislikes?' The fact that the words are different genders may not have registered with the students. If not much attention is drawn to gender at other times during the course, learners will never appreciate its significance, with the result that learning the correct endings for adjectives, relative pronouns, etc will be much more difficult for class members later on.

Occasionally carry out a listening exercise where the aim is to concentrate on the small differences in sound between grammatical points. Try supplying a written transcript of a listening text with the articles or adjective endings blanked out to encourage students to hear whether it is *le, la* or *les, piccolo* or *piccola, gute* or *gutes*, etc. In the early stages of language courses, or if you have less able students, be sure not to turn this exercise into too much of an old-fashioned dictation where students do not hear differences in endings but have to use their knowledge of grammar to enable them to answer, e.g. they hear '*aller*' but is it spelt *aller, allez, allais, allait, allaient, allé, allée, allés* or *allées*? The aim is to improve their intensive listening skills.

Getting the gender wrong in German can often lead to ambiguity, e.g. *der Fehler* — (only one) mistake, *die Fehler* — mistakes (plural). To encourage learners to recognise differences in the definite article, conduct an oral exercise asking students to tell you whether you say the singular form first or second:

>   die Brüder   der Bruder
>   der Wagen   die Wagen
>   der Onkel   die Onkel

Alternatively, ask students to tell you which is the odd one out (as far as the article is concerned) in a group of words you read out:

> le fromage   le pain   la viande   le vin
> le marché   le parc   le cinéma   les magasins

Of course, the odd mistake in gender is not a serious error and we do not want learners to become inhibited about speaking for fear of making errors, but slotting in an occasional gender awareness exercise will make life much easier later on, since so much else in the language depends on it.

Over to you

Task   What aspects of grammar do learners find difficult in your language? Why? If your learners' native language is English, is it English usage that is misleading them? Devise some activities or exercises which highlight the correct use of these structures.

Allow learners to discover rules for themselves

Learning is an active process, we do not automatically retain facts just because someone tells us. How many times have you switched on the radio specifically to catch the weather forecast and then, when the forecast is over, you realise that you did not hear a word? This is because it is hard to concentrate on intensive listening, you can be easily distracted and even when you think you **are** listening, the words frequently wash over you and you cannot recall them later.

If a tutor introduces a grammatical structure by explaining how to form it, for example, by saying 'take the *nous* form of the present tense, knock off the *-ons* and add the endings *-ais, -ais, -ait,* etc to form the imperfect', she or he cannot be sure that all the class was listening to the explanation, nor that everyone has understood it, regardless of how easy it seems to those of us who know French. The more able learners may well grasp the rules and be able to apply them to a range of verbs, but others will flounder.

Most people learn by doing things for themselves. After all, isn't this how we help our own children to learn skills — they have to be given the time and space to try and tie their own shoelaces, use a knife and fork and fasten buttons? We may feel frustrated looking on and know the job would get done in a fraction of the time if we did it ourselves, but we are doing our children no favours in the long run if we do not let them learn by their own efforts. As the old adage goes, practice makes perfect.

By putting into practice other strategies mentioned in this book, such as taking one new thing at a time and letting learners hear plenty of carefully chosen examples of a new language structure, the rules will gradually become apparent. What happens in practice is this: imagine I am introducing the accusative case for the first time in a German Level 1 class. The first time I say '*Ich möchte einen . . .*' learners will be surprised to hear the new form and may feel at a loss to know why. As I go on giving more and more examples, learners will mentally form a hypothesis, they will think they know what is causing the ending to change. One learner may think 'Oh, I see, after *möchte* you have to say *einen*'. He then begins to test this hypothesis. If I say '*Ich möchte eine Tasse Tee*', the learner will realise his hypothesis is false, so he will start considering other possibilities, maybe 'Ah, *eine* doesn't change just *ein*'. When I say '*Ich möchte ein Bier*' he will realise that that is wrong too, so he will try out another hypothesis 'Maybe it is only masculine nouns that change from *ein* to *einen*'. Every example now will reinforce this hypothesis and convince him that he has, in fact, established the rule.

Learners reach the stage at which the penny drops at different times, although extra examples will do no-one any harm, but when they do eventually get there it will be as a result of their own efforts.

When the class have all reached the 'Aha, I see' stage, **then** recap on what has happened to the word endings and, just as important, **why** it has happened. It is important, from the tutor's point of view, to be sure that learners have understood correctly and, from the learners' point of view, to have their hypothesis and theory validated, so they do not go home from the lesson in any doubt. If your preparation was thorough and your presentation clear and systematic, you will find that learners will have grasped the rules and you will only have to label them — 'We call this the accusative case' or 'This is the object of the verb'. Give your learners a pat on the back for working the rules out for themselves and let them feel a sense of achievement which will help maintain their motivation.

Only teach what learners need to know now

We need to remind ourselves constantly why people enrol for our classes. In most cases learners wish to use the language for business or holiday purposes, they primarily want to be able to find out information, chat to people, sell to them and so on. They need to know language that will help them achieve their objectives. They do not need to be told umpteen ways of saying the same thing, be given a long list of exceptions to every rule, nor do they need to be taught language that is more appropriate for a literary style.

Most learners will rarely need to write any formal documents in the foreign language in their working or private lives, so they will not find an in-depth knowledge of the past historic tense in French, for instance, particularly useful. In the early years of language courses learners will probably not need to write much at all in the target language outside the classroom, so it makes sense not to devote a disproportionate amount of time at this stage to teaching grammatical points that are more appropriate for the written language than the spoken. The preceding direct object rule in French (*'la lettre que j'ai lue'*) is an example of this; you cannot hear the extra *e* in the spoken language so, if speaking is the main goal of your students, there is no need to use up valuable lesson time giving exercises on past participle agreement, although you will probably briefly draw attention to it when it comes up in context, so that learners will recognise it.

There are only a certain amount of hours in a language course and you cannot teach everything. If you decide to devote more time to one thing, e.g. past participle agreement, you will have to devote less time to something else. As a tutor you must decide on your priorities, and these will depend on your learners' priorities which may well be different in different classes.

It is unfair and patronising to answer a learner's question by saying 'Oh, don't worry about that' or 'You don't need to know that'. Once a learner has asked a question on something that has cropped up in a lesson, you must answer, albeit briefly.

If you do not want to get drawn into discussions and explanations on certain structures because they are too advanced for the class, make sure they do not crop up in the lesson accidentally. Careful planning is vital here; have plenty of examples up your sleeve which do not include irregularities or difficult grammar that you want to leave until a later date. Exceptions or extensions to the rule we are teaching are more likely to surface in your lesson when you are trying to think of examples 'off the cuff'.

Of course, the exceptions to the rule or the more difficult grammatical structures will be taught eventually, possibly within a few weeks, possibly not for another year or so. The point is, you do not need to introduce everything at once, only teach what learners need to know **at that particular stage**. Most tutors, for instance, would have their students using *'je voudrais'*, *'ich möchte'*, 'I would like' right from the first few weeks of a course, just treating it as an item of vocabulary. It will be some time before the conditional is taught in its entirety.

Many structures can be avoided, and alternatives used instead. Learners will still be able to say what they want. I would delay the introduction of the genitive case in a German Level 1 class for as long as possible. English speakers usually have enough problems with accusative and dative case endings. Instead, I would use *von*, e.g. *die Schwester von meinem Mann*. Similarly, in everyday speech, Germans are far more likely to use the *würde* form to say 'would', so apart from the commonly used *hätte, wäre, möchte* and other modals, it is not worth learners struggling with the imperfect subjunctive in German — *ich käme, er täte*, etc.

French people are more likely to say *'Vous vous êtes levé à quelle heure?'* than *'A quelle heure vous êtes-vous levé?'*, so avoid teaching the complicated word order of the latter form and concentrate on the more straightforward word order to start with.

Remember you cannot teach everything at once, you have to prioritise.

How much grammatical terminology to use

The use of the correct terminology, e.g. verbs, adjectives, relative pronouns is a helpful shortcut when explaining structures in the foreign language **if** the class understands it. The difficulty is in knowing what terminology is understood by your class and what is not. Asking your class 'Who doesn't know what a verb is?' will probably not give you the answer you need, as adults do not like appearing ignorant in front of others. On the other hand, to say 'doing words' every time you want to use the word 'verbs' sounds contrived. It is usually better to assume that no-one knows the terminology and when you first introduce the words, explain them in the students' own language and give plenty of examples. Or, check knowledge of grammatical terms by asking direct questions such as 'Does anyone know what we call words like he, me, it which we use to avoid repeating certain words as in the sentence I know that man, that man is called John?' Explanations of terminology can often get long and unwieldy; usually the best way to help learners is to provide plenty of examples.

It must be remembered that many English speakers are not familiar with words like 'adjective', 'indirect object', 'genitive', etc. If you mention these words, such learners immediately switch off, sure that what you are about to say will be beyond them, and no matter how simply and sympathetically you explain, they will not be listening. Using techniques and strategies mentioned elsewhere in this book, such as colour coding, clear illustration and presentation of one set of endings at a time, will help you keep your use of grammatical terminology to a minimum.

It is quite in order to define and then use basic terms such as verb, adjective, noun, pronoun, subject and object. If you are teaching an inflected language, the names of cases (accusative, dative, etc) will be useful to learners. Be guided by the terminology that appears in the coursebook you are using. The coursebooks *BBC Russian language and people* and *Ruslan,* for example, describe verbs as being either first or second conjugation, *Breakthrough Russian,* another commonly used textbook, does not use those terms. *The French Experience* uses little grammatical terminology in each unit, although such terms as demonstrative and object pronouns do come up in the language summary at the back of the book. Do you expect your students to read this section? If so, use the terminology, but many learners will not read it, unless you specifically advise them to.

Where there are alternative names for particular terms, use the ones mentioned in the coursebook, so as not to confuse learners, or at least give them the various options and say they mean the same thing. Learners may be confused if you constantly refer to disjunctive pronouns when their coursebook (*The French Experience,* for example) calls them emphatic pronouns.

Use your discretion as to whether you use the target language or English when you explain. Cognates such as *masculin, féminin, Genitiv, verbo* and *adjectivo* will be understood in the target language, but where the vocabulary is very different from English, it is preferable to use English with all classes except for advanced groups. After all, it is difficult enough learning useful everyday Russian without being faced with the rather terrifying *eemya sushchestveetelnoye* and *eemya preelagatelnoye* (noun and adjective)!

Several years ago when I was first learning to play bridge a more experienced friend stood behind me. She usually shook her head at the card I picked out and pointed out another one, which I dutifully put down. I may have made my three no trumps contract, but I was none the wiser as to how to play bridge.

Treat correction of errors as part of the learning process

In order to learn from their mistakes, learners need to understand **why** they got something wrong. Just saying the correct form yourself, even if you ask learners to repeat the correct version after you, will not necessarily stop them making the same mistake the next time they want to use that structure. It is better to encourage learners to use their cognitive powers to correct their errors themselves, so that they do not just mindlessly repeat a phrase, which they may or may not understand.

Imagine a learner has just said '*L'année dernière j'ai allé en France*' in answer to a question. You say '*L'année dernière je . . .*' and pause with a quizzical look on your face; this lets the learner know he has made a mistake. Now he has to stop and ask himself **why** the next word was wrong. If the teaching point of that or a recent lesson is verbs taking *être*, the learner will realise that he had just forgotten that *aller* is not an *avoir* verb, and he will correct himself without a single word from the tutor. Having worked it out for himself, he is more likely to remember it.

A suitable facial expression or gesture from the tutor is usually enough to indicate that an error has been made. If a learner misses off an ending I cup my hand around my ear to show that not all the word is there, or I put my hands in front of me, palms facing, fingers pointing forward, about twenty centimetres apart then gently move them further apart and back again as if I were stretching something between my hands, with the aim, again, of showing that the word needs a little bit more added.

Distinguish between errors that are slips of the tongue caused by insufficient oral practice, and errors caused by an actual lack of understanding. If they are trying to say several sentences at a time — perhaps you have just asked them to describe their last holiday — learners may make quite basic errors in gender or word order which they would not make if the situation was more controlled and at a slower pace. Constantly pulling up learners for such errors, for instance, reminding a German class that the past participle should go at the end of the sentence, will be counter-productive. They know that already, it is just that with trying to concentrate on fluency, their mouths were working faster than their brains and the errors just slipped out!

Tutors can offer far more help to learners if they realise **why** learners make particular mistakes; a knowledge of the native English speaker's way of thinking and thus what is likely to cause difficulty in the foreign language is very useful here. Many learners will not recognise that the word 'work' is a different part of speech in each of the three phrases 'he is at work', 'I work in London' and 'I must buy some new work clothes'. Just correcting the ending is not enough; more advice on recognising verbs, adjectives and nouns is advisable (c.f. 'Encourage grammatical awareness among learners', p8).

A typical error for the learner is to answer the question '*Wo wohnen Sie?*' or '*Où travaillez-vous?*' with '*Ich wohnen . . .*' and '*Je travaillez . . .*' The learner has been affected by what he has heard. If you just repeat the correct version, it may not register; sometimes learners do not hear small differences in sound. It is better to draw the learner's attention to **why** he has made the error, so that he can make a conscious effort in the future to change the ending. As well as using a gesture, as mentioned above, this can easily be done using the target language:

Tutor: *Wo wohnen Sie?*
Learner: *Ich wohnen in Guildford*
Tutor: ***Sie* wohn*en*, *ich* . . ?**, with a quizzical look and emphasising *Sie* and verb ending to show that they go together.

If the learner does not come up with *wohne,* give it yourself, emphasising the ending. Give a few more examples, if necessary, contrasting the *ich* and *Sie* forms for verbs that have already been covered during the course.

Often the clue to the correct form to be used in the answer is in the question. Learners may miss this as they are too busy concentrating on the meaning of the question and thinking how they are going to reply, rather than registering the details. A learner of English might reply 'I am living in Guildford for six months', even though the correct verb form 'have been living' was in the question. Gently remind learners that if they listen carefully, half the work is done for them. Occasionally conduct activities which develop listening skills, as mentioned earlier in 'Encourage grammatical awareness among learners' (p9).

Fluency is a skill in its own right. Treat fluency and grammatical accuracy, therefore, as separate skills, each with its own best way of being developed and improved. When learners are involved in tasks which are designed to develop fluency, e.g. group work, games, class surveys, pair work, it will not help them achieve this objective if you constantly stop the activity to correct grammatical errors. Do not embark on a freer, student-centred activity until you have thoroughly practised the new structure in a controlled situation and are sure that the class has grasped it.

Operate a priority system when correcting errors in class. Interrupting a learner every few words to correct a gender or an ending is demotivating and inhibits the shyer students from saying anything. Top priority should be the particular grammatical structure you are concentrating on at the time. Then come mistakes where learners mean one thing but say another, for example when someone says '*J'aime une bouteille de vin*' when they should have said '*Je voudrais*', or someone who says '*mon fils*' when they really mean '*mes fils*'. If there are one or two people in the class who make very few errors in the new structure, you might make more comments to them on other, smaller errors, so that you are perceived to be treating people equally and it is not just a handful of people being corrected all the time.

Over to you

Task Think of a grammatical structure you will be teaching soon. How will you teach it? What will you start with? Are there any irregular forms you want to avoid mentioning? Can you think up a context to present the language where you will not have to explain using grammatical terminology?

Techniques
Chapter 3

Learners are all different; they all have different learning styles. There is, therefore, no one 'best' way to teach a particular grammatical structure. The examples I give in this book have worked for me and my students; they are in no way designed to be prescriptive. Success will depend on the learners' needs and their preferred learning methods as well as the tutor's own personality and teaching style. The best approach to take is to be flexible and offer plenty of variety. If one suggestion does not work for you, do not write it off completely, try it again at a later date, with another group or with minor amendments. If you are still not happy, just try something else!

The brain can only process so much new information at one time. New language structures should, therefore, be introduced one at a time, with learners being given plenty of opportunity to assimilate and consolidate these structures before moving on.

Take one thing at a time

If you are planning to introduce the partitive article (*du, de la, de l', des*) early on in a French beginners' course, do not overwhelm the students with lists of new vocabulary to do with food and drink that same lesson. Instead, attach *du, de la,* etc to items that have already come up in the course. More vocabulary can be introduced a lesson or two later, providing a good opportunity to revise the recently learnt partitive article.

It is, of course, vital to plan lessons several weeks in advance; you can then make sure that you have covered vocabulary which contains words of all genders, words beginning with a vowel, singulars and plurals, etc depending on your language and the language structure concerned.

Most classes can manage the partitive article in French or the accusative case of nouns in German or Russian in one lesson, but there are some grammatical structures which, themselves, need to be broken up into smaller, more manageable chunks of language and presented to the class bit by bit.

Tenses will usually fall into this category. For learners' first exposure to the past tense start by presenting just one type of verb, such as regular *-er* verbs in French, *-ar* verbs in Spanish or regular weak verbs in German and think up contexts where a range of verbs of this type can be presented. Discussing what you did last week is a good way of using the past tense and a full, varied 'diary' can be built up using verbs such as *jouer* (a good opportunity to revise sports vocabulary), *regarder, visiter, travailler, acheter, dîner*. Note that the verbs chosen for each language will be different. German, too, could start off with *spielen, arbeiten, kaufen,* but, since you want to give plenty of examples of the pattern *ge...t,* it would be best not to mention *besuchen* or any verbs with prefixes at this stage. Advance planning and forethought is necessary to ensure that you do not accidentally slip in a verb which does not follow the same rules exactly, e.g. a verb taking *être, essere* or *sein*, separable verbs, reflexives.

The context can be varied to suit the particular needs of your class; for a business French class you could use verbs describing office activities, e.g. *envoyer, téléphoner, réserver, copier, travailler, déjeuner, annuler, rencontrer, commander*.

Simplifying your introduction of new language in this way and keeping it very structured will ensure that your students gradually see a pattern in what you are saying. You can then start bringing in other verbs of the same type (e.g. *écouter, manger, machen, hören*), but this time **you** will not put them into the past tense, the students will. If they get it right, this will show that they have recognised the pattern and are now able to apply the rule successfully to other verbs. Now you can move on, perhaps by introducing some irregular verbs, or another conjugation, then those taking *être* or *essere*. In German I like to continue with strong verbs that still have the prefix *ge-* (*essen, trinken, lesen,* etc) before moving to inseparable verbs, then verbs taking *sein* and finally separable verbs.

Even more advanced classes will welcome new language structures being introduced in a controlled and systematic manner. When introducing the conditional in German, which uses a subjunctive in both halves of the sentence, start off by asking students to cope with one verb in the subjunctive at a time, keeping the *wenn* clause constant, e.g.:

Learner 1: *Wenn ich eine Million Pfund hätte, würde ich ein neues Haus kaufen.*
Learner 2: *Wenn ich eine Million Pfund hätte, würde ich eine Weltreise machen.*
Learner 3: *Wenn ich eine Million Pfund hätte, würde ich meine Arbeitsstelle aufgeben.*

Gradually introduce other examples in the *wenn* clause to give more practice:

Was würden Sie machen, wenn Sie mehr Freizeit hätten?
Was würden Sie machen, wenn Sie Premierminister wären?
Was würden Sie machen, wenn Sie nicht arbeiteten?

. . . until eventually learners can handle the whole of complex sentences such as:

Wenn ich die Lotterie gewinnen würde, würde ich eine Jacht kaufen.

Relate the new to the known

Just as we find it easier to learn and assimilate something when it is presented to us bit by bit in a logical manner, so we find it easier to understand and remember something when we can relate it to something we already know. A class of English speakers will find the French words *oignons* and *carottes* easier to remember than the German words for the same items. *Zwiebel* and *Möhren* are much less like the English, so are harder to remember.

Learners will find it easier to get their German adjectival endings right after *ein/eine*, for example, if their attention is drawn to the fact that the endings *ein gut**er** Mann, eine gut**e** Frau, ein gut**es** Kind* end in *r*, *e* and *s*, just like *der, die* and *das*.

The position of object pronouns in French often causes difficulty for English speakers (e.g. *je vous donne, il m'a dit*), and in the early days learners may forget to put them before the verb or find the whole concept a difficult one to grasp. If this is the case, remind learners of the common phrase *s'il vous plaît* and point out the function and position of the word *vous*. When you introduce the dative case of personal pronouns in German, remind learners that they have been using *mir* and *Ihnen* very successfully since Lesson One when they learnt *Wie geht es Ihnen?* and *Es geht mir gut*.

The conditional tense in French becomes a lot less of a hurdle if you tell learners that they are already familiar with the verb's stem from their study of the future tense and with the ending from their study of the imperfect tense.

When introducing the passive voice to a German class, stress that it holds no terrors, based as it is on two things well known to the class — the past participle and the verb *werden*.

Expose learners to unknown grammar in natural situations

As babies, we **hear** language before we attempt to produce it. Foreign language learners also benefit from hearing as much of the target language as possible, even if more advanced grammatical structures are used than learners are capable of actually producing themselves at the time. Provided that what you say is comprehensible, and as you will often accompany the language by gestures or the context will be clear, learners **will** understand the overall gist of what you say.

So, for instance, you might draw three columns on the whiteboard, then show a sheet of paper to the students and say in the foreign language 'Draw three columns on a sheet of paper'. Similarly, as you hand out role cards you could say to individuals 'You will be the shop assistant', 'You will be the customer'.

Learners will have a head start when the structure in question is actually introduced formally. You could use the following expressions frequently in class depending on your language — '*Avete finito?*', '*Qui a fini?*', '*Quelle réponse avez-vous choisi?*', '*Haben Sie verstanden?*' or '*Was haben Sie geschrieben?*' Each time these phrases are spoken the correct form is heard and is gradually being absorbed by the learners, so that when they come to produce sentences in the past tense for themselves, they will already be familiar with the pattern.

The aim of using the target language as much as possible is to increase learners' confidence and benefit them; it is not meant to demotivate and demoralise. Choose what you say carefully where unknown grammatical structures are concerned; ask yourself 'Will learners understand this? Is the context clear?' Long-winded explanations given in the target language using jargon and grammatical terminology may not meet these criteria.

Illustrate and demonstrate, don't explain

Learners will perceive your lessons as more relevant if you illustrate or demonstrate what the language can be used **for**, rather than explain **about** the language. If students are meeting the dative case for the first time in the phrase '*Wie komme ich zum/ zur . . ?*' they may well lose interest or become anxious if you immediately mention the word dative, explain how the preposition combines with the definite article and then changes according to gender. It is better to introduce the lesson by saying that by the end of the evening everyone will be able to ask the way to places around town in Germany. Learners will immediately see that this is a useful bit of language to know, it is relevant to their needs and so they will be motivated to carry on listening. Similarly, rather than tell your French class that you are going to practise the imperfect tense (*Si on allait au cinéma?*), it is far more motivating and interesting to say that they are going to learn how to make suggestions.

Many adults, if they have been brought up in Britain, will never have been taught grammatical terminology at school, so there is little point in your explaining grammatical structures technically and expecting your class to understand. Some learners will think that they are the only ones in the class not to understand and will be too inhibited to ask.

Avoid giving long complicated explanations of grammatical structures describing tense formations, subordinate clauses and so on, but make it clear what you are referring to by the use of illustrations, demonstration, gestures and other techniques.

Do not start off the lesson when you intend to introduce the past tense by saying 'Now we're going to learn the *passé composé*' or something similar. If learners have already met the word *hier, gestern,* etc then, by using it in your examples, it will be obvious you are talking about the past. You can point to today's date on a calendar, then to yesterday's to make it clear what tense you are referring to. A copy of last week's pages from a diary will show you are referring to what you did last week and writing up 1996, 1995, etc when describing a holiday will imply you are talking about the past.

It does not matter what sort of codes, symbols or gestures you use in your lesson to illustrate various grammatical points, nor does it matter if other teachers use something entirely different. What is important is that you are consistent, i.e. always use the same gesture to mean the same thing and that your students recognise what you mean. I like to point back over my shoulder with my thumb to show that I am referring to the past, to point at or tap vigorously on my watch to refer to 'now' and to make a big, sweeping forward pointing gesture to refer to the future.

Colour coding your visual material is a very effective way of highlighting genders, tense forms, etc without having to keep pointing them out explicitly. The advantage of such 'props' is that students can take the support offered if they need it, but the more able students who **do** know the correct genders and tense forms can just ignore the background colour.

You must be consistent if you choose to go down this route; you cannot just choose whatever piece of card you happen to have available at the time. You need to start thinking about a colour coding system right from the start of the course.

When you introduce vocabulary, stick the picture or draw the symbol on a flashcard, a different colour for each gender. Learners may not remember that *Kirche* is feminine, but they will know that if it's on yellow card, say, they should say '*eine*' rather than '*ein*' or '*Wie komme ich **zur*** . . .' not '*zum*'. For a student of English as a foreign language who finds it confusing to remember which form of the verb should be used in past tense questions, words such as see, stay, buy, eat, drink written on one colour card and saw, stayed, bought, ate, drank on another colour will help — if it's a question beginning 'Did you . . ?', it must be a pink word.

English-speaking students of German can often cope with the idea that verbs are sent to the end of the clause after certain words; the difficulty is that they often do not know which word in the clause is the verb. Writing out a sentence with the verb written in a different colour will help learners who are not sure what a verb is and they will not be embarrassed to answer questions in class.

Writing, drawing or sticking pictures on to bits of different colour card **is** time consuming, admittedly, but the same effect can be achieved by using different colour pens on an OHT or whiteboard, by underlining or by drawing a box around the verb.

Of course, the use of colour coding in class is only a temporary prop and will not stop learners making mistakes in the country of the target language when they try to speak. The primary purpose of the props and techniques I have mentioned in this section is to give learners confidence in class and reinforce the correct version. If learners say the correct gender along with the noun enough times, it will hopefully stick, just as they will no doubt see *ist, gibt, war, hat* highlighted so often that they will eventually immediately recognise them as verbs.

'Time lines' can often clarify the meaning of a particular tense better than a verbal explanation, e.g.:

I did, *j'ai fait* . . .

I used to do, *je faisais* . . .

I have been doing, *je fais . . . depuis* . . .

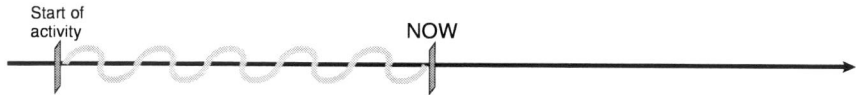

I was doing . . . when something happened, *je faisais . . . quand quelque chose s'est passé*

Everyone has a different learning style; what is a crystal clear explanation for one person is incomprehensible to another. If one technique does not clarify the meaning of certain structures for some learners, try another.

Make it fun

Learning to speak a language correctly demands time, effort and commitment. Verb and adjective endings and other grammatical forms still need to be learnt and practised extensively, even if you have abandoned the grammar-focused teaching methods of the past. Learners appreciate activities which practise grammatical structures more if they are short, snappy, contain an element of unpredictability and are enjoyable.

Revising verb endings by playing a dice-throwing game satisfies all the above criteria. On an ordinary die cover the dots with stickers, on which are written one of the six personal pronouns of the verb — *je, tu, il/elle,* etc (you can also buy ready printed dice for your language). On a separate pile of cards are pin drawings representing different verbs, or you can just write the infinitive if you prefer — you have to do this anyway for verbs like 'to have, know, want' which are difficult to represent pictorially (again, you can buy ready produced cards depicting actions and activities). Turn the pile of cards face downwards and divide the class into groups of three or four. One person in each group throws the die and turns over a verb card. The task is to put the correct ending on to that verb, depending on the side of the die which is uppermost. So if the card depicts 'to run' and the die lands on *nous,* the players have to say '*Nous courons*'. Make sure you tell learners in advance whether they are to take turns or whether the aim is to be the first in the group to come up with the correct form. As the tutor cannot be everywhere at once, advise learners to correct each others' mistakes; you might suggest they look up the correct version in the grammar section of their coursebook or a verb reference book if they are still not sure of the correct form. Obviously, you will have made clear to the class which tense they are to practise if it is not immediately obvious from whatever you are teaching at the time. In this game it does not matter whether some groups are faster than others and finish the pile of cards first. The cards can just keep being turned over and over and the chances are that next time round a different person in the group will have to put a different ending on a different verb. Ten minutes is usually enough for this activity, but it can be played every few weeks or even more often if the class need and enjoy it, and the verb cards can be changed each time to allow you to bring in recently learnt verbs or more irregular examples.

Giving learners the opportunity to think about what they are saying and to use their imaginations — even let them run riot — can take the boring predictability out of traditional grammar exercises and ensure everyone has fun which, in turn, will make the structures easier to remember.

Below are some ideas for activities whose aim is to practise specific grammatical structures, but in enjoyable, lively or amusing contexts.

In the traditional game each player has to add a noun each time (my grandmother went to market and bought some plums, some lemons, a water melon, etc). The same principle can be used to practise verbs:

Variation on My grandmother went to market

Hier je suis allé à Londres.
Hier je suis allé à Londres et j'ai visité Buckingham Palace.
Hier je suis allé à Londres, j'ai visité Buckingham Palace et j'ai vu Big Ben.
Hier je suis allé à Londres, j'ai visité Buckingham Palace, j'ai vu Big Ben et j'ai déjeuné à l'hôtel Ritz. [1]

. . . and so on.

Any tense can be practised here. Say you wanted to find an activity to practise the English present perfect. In pairs one partner says he or she has just done something and the other person has to go one better. The tutor can make the first statement if preferred and throw it open to the group or it can be played around the class like *My grandmother went to market,* with each class member trying to outdo his neighbour.

Going one better

I've just come back from Bournemouth.
Well, I've just come back from the Seychelles.

I've just been skiing.
Well, I've just been white-water rafting.

I've just bought a new Ford Escort.
Well, I've just bought a Rolls Royce.

The above two activities include all the elements of a grammar drill — plenty of repetition in a highly structured exercise. However, learners have an element of choice over what they say — it could be totally ridiculous — and so they are not just repeating words mindlessly.

---

1. This and similar games are described in *Language games and activities* by John Langran and Sue Purcell (CILT, 1994).

28 Teaching grammar communicatively

Awkward waiters (hotel receptionists, shopkeepers, etc)

This is a useful activity in any language which requires a different structure when using the negative 'I/we haven't got . . .' It is performed in pairs or with the teacher taking the role of the customer.

Customer: У вас есть пиво? (Vous avez de la bière?)

Waiter: Пива нет. (Nous n'avons pas de bière)

Customer: У вас есть борщ?

Waiter: Борща нет.

To practise German word order in indirect questions, there could be an awkward suspect being questioned by the police . . .

Police officer: *Wie heißen Sie?*
Suspect: *Ich will/ kann nicht sagen, wie ich heiße.*

Police officer: *Wo waren Sie gestern um 10 Uhr?*
Suspect: *Ich will/ kann nicht sagen, wo ich gestern um 10 Uhr war.*

. . . or an extremely unhelpful person, answering every question with 'Ich weiß nicht, . . . '

Wo sind meine Bücher?
Ich weiß nicht, wo Ihre Bücher sind.

Wer war letzte Woche nicht hier?
Ich weiß nicht, wer letzte Woche nicht hier war.

Here the second partner does not have the freedom to use vocabulary of his or her own choice; their role is purely to manipulate language. But if the partners swap roles halfway through the activity, they will both get the opportunity to think up questions, either out of their own head or from prompts (drawings, symbols or key words) supplied by the tutor.

The situations are, of course, not those that a learner will ever necessarily find him or herself in when abroad and I am certainly not suggesting that a learner should be awkward and unhelpful. Nevertheless, the exercises are useful as well as amusing since the language being practised is relevant to lots of different contexts.

Surveys

A survey can be devised to give extensive oral practice of a particular tense as well as to facilitate learner interaction. You could devise a set of questions for learners to put to their classmates to practise the present perfect tense, for example:

> 1 Find someone who has been to South America.
> 2 Find someone who has lived in the same town all his/her life.
> 3 Find someone who has eaten snails.
> 4 Find someone who has travelled on Eurostar.
> 5 Find someone who has read *David Copperfield*.

Lay down the ground rules, e.g. learners cannot use the same person as answer to more than two questions, revise the question and answer forms learners will use and give them fifteen or twenty minutes to try and put a name next to each question. As well as this being an activity which focuses extensively on one tense, it contributes to group dynamics by making for a friendly relaxed atmosphere.

Over to you

Task Instead of saying to learners 'Tonight we're doing the conditional/comparatives/prepositions which can take the accusative and dative', can you think of ways of describing the grammar points you teach in terms of their function, e.g. 'Tonight I want you to imagine winning the lottery. What would you buy?'

Examples of presentation of grammar points

Chapter 4

Simple past tense in English

Set the scene, showing OHT 1 below:

OHT 1

4. Examples of presentation of grammar points 31

Revise the verbs you intend to use later by saying something on the lines of 'I am a creature of habit, I lead a very boring life, I do the same things every evening: I arrive home at six o'clock, I work in the garden, I phone my mother, I play tennis and I watch television'. These verbs should all be known and will cause no problems in the present tense.

Allow learners to revise these verbs in the present tense either by leaving up the same OHT and asking 'What do I do every day?' or asking them about themselves, e.g. 'What time do you arrive home after work?', 'What do you usually watch on television?', 'What sport do you play?', etc. If you prefer, show another OHT (see OHT 2) and ask learners to imagine that they, too, do the same things every day. Elicit from them 'I arrive home at half past five, I phone my father/brother . . . , I play golf/tennis and I listen to the radio/watch television'.

OHT 2

This introductory part of the lesson should be treated as a brief warm-up session. Try and encourage learners to use the regular verbs you will be concentrating on later when you introduce the past tense — some will try and say things like 'I get home at . . .'; do not make a big issue out of it if an irregular verb is used in this phase — it does not have to feature later on in the lesson.

Introduce the past form by saying 'I do these things every day and I did them yesterday too'. Show the first OHT again with an overlay which shows yesterday's date, whatever that was, and go through all the verbs on the acetate — yesterday I arrived home at six o'clock, I worked in the garden, etc.

4. *Examples of presentation of grammar points* 33

Encourage learners to practise this form by saying 'I arrived home at six o'clock last night, and you?', 'I watched *Panorama* on television, and you?' This question format means that learners will not yet be exposed to the question form of the past tense 'What **did** you . . . watch?'

Continue the oral practice using the same verbs for a bit longer, then, when you feel that learners have grasped the new ending, bring in more verbs of this type, for example, by asking questions such as 'I started/finished work today at six o'clock, and you?', 'I listened to Radio 4 this morning, and you?' Since learners will only be producing this one form in their answer, there is no harm in letting them hear the question form 'What did you watch?', 'What time did you start . . ?', 'Did you watch the television or listen to the radio this morning?' At this stage it might be a good idea to show the written form of the past tense. Another overlay can be used (see below).

Before you show the written form, you might like to ask learners what they notice about how they talk about things they did 'yesterday', i.e. elicit the 'rule' from them. They will probably say something like 'you add a 'd' sound', as they have not yet been exposed to the spellings. Praise the learners and give them a few more examples so that they can 'prove' the rule.

By now it should be quite clear to the class that you are talking about past events, so more verbs can be introduced and practised, even irregular ones. Equip students to be able to perform a freer, communicative activity later. When preparing your lesson, you will have thought up a suitable activity to practise and consolidate the new language structure, so bearing this activity in mind, make sure you introduce verbs that will feature within it. You may, for instance, want learners to talk simply about their last holiday, or play a guessing game trying to guess where other people went on holiday. In this case the past forms 'went, ate, drank, bought, spoke' might be useful ('Last year I went to Russia, I ate caviar, I drank vodka, I bought a samovar and I spoke Russian'). You will also need to highlight the question form for the guessing game ('Did you speak French? Did you drink Chianti?', etc). Only introduce as many new verbs as learners can cope with.

Note that very little grammatical terminology was used during the presentation of this new grammatical structure; it was quite clear that learners were talking about the past thanks to the use of visuals, notably yesterday's date. Only known regular verbs of one type were used to start off with until it was quite clear that learners were able to apply those endings to other examples. Feedback was obtained by asking learners questions using the new forms, they discovered the rule for forming the past tense of regular verbs for themselves and by the end of the lesson they were using the language in a natural, relevant situation.

Over to you

Task 1 If you were introducing a past tense in your language what changes would you make to your initial OHT? Which of the verbs 'arrive, work, play, phone, watch, listen' would you **not** introduce at this initial stage and which other verbs might you use instead? Has an exception to the rule accidentally slipped in?

Task 2 If you were teaching a specialist business language class what verbs could you use in your introductory section that would be relevant to the needs of your learners?

If this is your group's first encounter with a finite verb being sent to the end of the clause, stick to just one subordinating conjunction. I like to start with *weil* (meaning 'because') because I introduce it soon after the impersonal verb *gefallen* has been taught and it provides a good opportunity for revision of this verb.

Word order in subordinate clauses in German

Start off by asking your group of adult students '*Gefällt Ihnen Ihre Arbeit?*' ('Do you like your work?') and when they answer '*Ja*' or '*Nein*', ask '*Warum?*' and jot down the responses on the right hand half of the board or flip chart. If learners are reticent about coming out with ideas off the cuff or haven't had any warm-up, you can start talking about yourself to give them some ideas which they can apply to their own jobs, e.g. '*Meine Arbeit gefällt mir; meine Kollegen sind freundlich, ich arbeite nur morgens, ich habe ein schönes Büro, die Arbeit ist interessant. Manchmal gefällt mir meine Arbeit nicht; ich bekomme nicht viel Geld, ich muß viel zu Hause arbeiten, ich muß abends arbeiten, es gibt keine Kantine*'. You may well end up with a board that looks similar to the following:

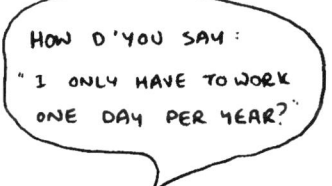

Meine Arbeit gefällt mir   meine Kollegen sind nett
　　　　　　　　　　　　　　　ich habe ein schönes Büro
　　　　　　　　　　　　　　　ich habe einen Firmenwagen
　　　　　　　　　　　　　　　die Arbeit ist interessant

Meine Arbeit gefällt mir nicht ich muß viel reisen
ich habe keine Sekretärin
die Arbeit ist langweilig
meine Stelle hat keine Zukunft

You can now start linking both halves of the sentence together with *weil*. Although slightly long-winded and artificial, it is best to make individual sentences for each phrase, e.g. *meine Arbeit gefällt mir, weil meine Kollegen nett sind; meine Arbeit gefällt mir, weil ich ein schönes Büro habe; meine Arbeit gefällt mir nicht, weil ich viel reisen muß* and so on. As you say each phrase, underline the verb you are sending to the end; this will be of help later to those learners who may forget which word in the clause is the verb. Return to your original questions — '*Warum gefällt Ihnen Ihre Arbeit (nicht)?*' — and let learners repeat their original reasons, but this time in a complex sentence containing *weil*.

Learners now need to practise using *weil* in more sentences and different contexts, but until they are confident about which word is the verb and are fluent enough to juggle the words around in their head, keep practising in a whole group situation, where you can control the language to be manipulated and can monitor their progress. One way is for you to provide 'reasons' for liking or disliking a job and learners to preface each reason with '*Meine Arbeit gefällt mir, weil . . .*' or '*Meine Arbeit gefällt mir nicht, weil . . .*' You can show pictures of various occupations to broaden the activity and learners can reply as if they had that occupation. You might show a picture of a postman, for instance, and give the prompts '*Ich muß eine Uniform tragen*' (or '*Ich trage eine Uniform*'), '*Ich muß sehr früh aufstehen*', '*Ich mag Hunde nicht*'. Note that there can be no right or wrong answers here; one person will enjoy wearing a uniform, another won't. The longer and more complicated the sentence, the more difficult learners will find it to remember to include all the words in the right order! More than one verb in the sentence (*. . . weil ich früh aufstehen muß, . . . weil ich zu viel zu tun habe*) will undoubtedly make the learners' task harder and you should grade your prompts accordingly, starting off with short simple phrases and gradually making your sentences longer. If you feel that some learners may not be able to identify the verb, you could give learners written support; have the sentences already written out with the verbs highlighted.

Learners have now extensively practised word order after *weil*, they have understood what they have been saying and they have assimilated the rule for themselves. If someone asks 'Why?' all you need to say is that a lot of words send verbs to the end in German (and learners are probably already familiar with modals sending the infinitive to the end), particularly words like *weil* which join two simple sentences to make a longer one and that such words are called conjunctions. Depending on how your class have performed so far, you can either bring in another subordinating conjunction or carry on using *weil* in a different context (talking about whether you like the town you live in, particular makes of cars, etc) Remember that a question beginning '*Warum?*' will require the use of *weil* in the answer, so some sort of game can be played where students have to think of a plausible answer to your '*Warum?*' questions, e.g.:

Warum gehen Sie nicht ins Kino mit uns? — weil ich kein Geld habe.
Warum gehen Sie zu Fuß heute? — weil mein Auto kaputt ist.
Warum schreiben Sie diese Worte nicht? — weil ich keinen Kuli habe.

Over to you

Task Word order is particularly relevant to German. Think up a context for extensive practice of another subordinating conjunction, e.g. *daß, obgleich*.

Direct object pronouns in French

In many coursebooks object pronouns are introduced quite late on, sometimes well after the introduction of past and future tenses. However, there is no reason why they should not be taught early on in a course, using the present tense only and vocabulary that is already known. Learners will then get used to the unfamiliar word order before being faced with more complex examples later on.

I like to introduce direct object pronouns shortly after students have learnt how to talk about their likes and dislikes, using, for instance *j'aime, j'aime beaucoup, j'aime assez, je n'aime pas tellement, je n'aime pas du tout* and *je déteste*.

I use vocabulary that is already known in my examples, so I might start off, for example, by saying:

J'aime le champagne, je l'aime beaucoup.

J'aime le sport, je l'aime un peu.
Je n'aime pas le whisky, je le déteste.
Je n'aime pas l'architecture moderne, je la déteste.
J'aime les Beatles, je les aime bien.
Je n'aime pas les escargots, je les déteste.

Stress the pronouns slightly more than you would in normal speech and give plenty of examples, so that learners gradually assimilate the rule. Do not present the pronouns in negative sentences just yet, i.e. avoid saying things like '*Je ne les aime pas tellement*', as there is a lot for learners to think about there; wait until the simple sentences come easily and automatically. Don't worry about the fact that *aimer* begins with a vowel and both *le* and *la* become *l'*; learners will get used to putting the pronoun in the correct position and other verbs can be brought in later.

Up to now learners have just heard the new structure, now it is their turn to produce it. Ask '*Vous aimez le . . ? vous aimez la . . ? vous aimez les . . ?*' using any vocabulary that will be understood, e.g. '*Vous aimez Max Bygraves? Vous aimez le métro à Londres? Vous aimez les Spice Girls?*' Try and use vocabulary which will arouse strong feelings to elicit a response rather than just a shrug of the shoulders. Alternatively, show an OHT (see below) depicting a character and various items (remember to include masculine, feminine and plural examples) and ask learners to answer from that person's point of view. *Aimer* and *détester* can both be indicated by symbols and *aimer, aimer un peu, aimer beaucoup* can be indicated using one, two or three ticks.

Do not worry if you cannot draw very well; learners are not being asked to guess what you have drawn, they will hear the words from you first, e.g. '*Vous aimez les hamburgers?*' All learners need to do is to see in which column there is something that looks like a beefburger.

When learners have had plenty of practice at producing *je l'aime, je la déteste,* etc it is a good idea to check that the rule has actually been absorbed by getting learners to provide the question to your answer.

Teacher *Non, je le déteste.*
Learner *Vous aimez le whisky?* (or Frank Sinatra, or *le rugby* or anything that is masculine and singular)

Once you can see that the rule has been assimilated, you can introduce a short, learner-centred pair work activity. I give each pair two piles of cards; one pile contains pictures of nouns (masculine, feminine, singular and plural) and the other shows either a smiley face or a miserable one.

Partner A picks up a card depicting a noun and asks, for example, '*Vous aimez la bière?*' Partner B picks up a card from the other pile and answers accordingly ('*Oui, je l'aime*'). You can dispense with the second pile of cards if you like and learners can give their own opinion. The only likely problem with this approach is that learners may feel that *détester* is too strong a word and will try and use *ne . . . pas* in their answer, which has not yet been covered.

Now negatives can be introduced and practised in a similar way. Use your previous OHT and use an overlay of differing numbers of crosses against each disliked item (✗ = *je n'aime pas tellement,* ✗✗ = *je n'aime pas* and ✗✗✗ = *je n'aime pas du tout*). Let students hear the new form from you several times first before you ask them to produce it:

Je n'aime pas tellement le football, je ne l'aime pas tellement.
Je n'aime pas du tout les hamburgers, je ne les aime pas du tout.

Try and remember what people said they disliked earlier on in the lesson (or jot down at the time who used *détester* with what) and ask them to elaborate on how much they dislike it.

Follow the same format as for the earlier part of the lesson. If everything went well earlier and the class quickly grasped the teaching point you may have decided to cut out the earlier pair work activity, in which case include it now.

This topic lends itself very well to exploitation in a class survey, so round off the session with this group activity. You might, for instance set the task of finding out which sports or games are most and least popular among the class members. Prepare a handout divided into columns (see below); at the top of each column draw a picture or symbol depicting a particular sport (or the words if you are afraid that the drawings may not be clear), then write learners' names down the left hand column (or students can write these in during the activity). Every class member must talk to everyone else asking '*Vous aimez le golf? Vous aimez la pêche?*', etc and answering '*Non, je ne l'aime pas. Oui, je l'aime beaucoup*', etc. When the activity has finished see if a consensus can be reached on which sport can be said to be the most popular and which the least. Try and introduce a variety of sports and games likely to appeal to different people or arouse strong feelings. If you want to use vocabulary that may be new, perhaps *échecs* or *boules* to give a plural example, make sure it was included on your OHT earlier for learners to practise.

	⛳	🎳	🚴	●●●	🎣	🏈
Mike	✓✓✓	✗✗	✗✗	✓	✗✗✗	✓
Yasmin	✗✗	✓	✓✓✓	✓✓	✗✗✗	✗✗✗

✓✓✓	aime beaucoup	✗	n'aime pas tellement
✓✓	aime (assez)	✗✗	n'aime pas
✓	aime un peu	✗✗✗	déteste

So far only two verbs have been used in examples. Other verbs can now be brought in as can other pronouns, e.g. *me, vous,* etc. Time expressions can be revised as well as object pronouns practised using everyday vocabulary such as '*Vous regardez la télévision le soir ou le matin? Vous lavez souvent la voiture?*' The introduction of the indirect object pronouns *lui* and *leur* can neatly follow on in this context, e.g. '*Vous téléphonez souvent à votre mère/vos parents?*' If *depuis* has already been covered examples containing *connaître* will give plenty of practice of *me, vous,* etc as well as *le, la, les,* e.g. '*Je vous connais depuis quatre mois*'.

Over to you

Task Imagine you have just covered the vocabulary for household chores (as in Unit 9 of the BBC coursebook *The French Experience*). How would you introduce direct object pronouns for the first time within this context? Think of plenty of examples to use the object pronouns *le, la* and *les* with such verbs as *faire, laver, nettoyer,* etc.

Possessive adjectives in German

It is in the early days of learning a language that care must be taken not to overload learners with too much jargon for grammatical structures; beginners need plenty of time to get used to unknown words and concepts. By the time more advanced grammatical structures are introduced, e.g. participles, subjunctive, conditional, you are left with serious students in your class who are used to different endings and who can accept the fact that a foreign language is not necessarily like English all the time.

Possessive adjectives (*mein, Ihr,* etc) will be introduced early on in a course, at a time when vocabulary is being built up as well as new structures being learnt. I like to use the context of the family since it includes examples of masculine, feminine, singular and plural endings.

I start off by showing a photograph of my two children. Luckily (from a language teaching point of view) I have a boy and a girl, which gives me plenty of scope for practising two genders. I say '*Ich habe zwei Kinder*', I point to the photo and say '*Das sind **meine** Kinder*'. It is unlikely that the word *Kinder* will not be understood, but if learners looked blank I would point to various people round the class, then to the photo saying '*Mann, Mann, Frau, Frau, Kind, Kinder*'; I also dig my finger into my chest when saying '*meine*'. I then continue, pointing from one to the other '*Das ist mein Sohn, das ist meine Tochter, mein Sohn heißt Rory, meine Tochter heißt Lizzie; mein Sohn ist acht Jahre alt, meine Tochter ist elf Jahre alt*'. *Heißen* and numbers have already come up in the course. I start building up a simple family tree on the board:

I then try and get learners to use '*mein Sohn*' and '*meine Tochter*' by asking '*Haben Sie Kinder?*' and '*Mein Sohn heißt Rory, wie heißt Ihr Sohn?*' Despite the fact that I am now using *Ihr*, a new word, I am not yet asking learners to produce anything other than *mein(e)* and I am giving clues as to how I want the question to be answered, so it is rarely misunderstood. Several people give the names and ages of their children, so there is plenty of repetition. Note that you will probably have to give plurals at this stage for people who want to say '*Ich habe zwei Söhne*'. Do not worry too much if someone does not use the correct ending in '*Ich habe **einen** Sohn*'. You may have had the accusative case in a previous lesson, in which case you can make more of an issue of it, but if learners have not yet met this new ending, say it yourself but encourage students to give short answers to your questions '*Haben Sie Kinder? Ja? Nein? Wie viele? Sohn oder Tochter?*'

Now either show more photos or add more names to your family tree by saying '*Das ist mein Mann/Bruder/Vater, das ist meine Schwester/*

Mutter/Großmutter' and again, give learners the opportunity to talk about their own family.

As the teaching point here is possessive adjectives, insist on the correct ending, ideally by letting learners know if they make a mistake and letting them give the correct version. Learners will not realise your teaching point is adjective endings, they will be more interested in the vocabulary; as you write it up on the board, write the masculines and feminines in separate columns so that you can head each column *mein* or *meine* and possibly have a plural column too headed *meine*. If you prefer, and depending on how you have treated the subject of gender so far, you can also write up *masculine* and *feminine* above the relevant columns.

I now wish to practise *Ihr*, so I ask one or two people in the class who mentioned they had children '*Wie heißt Ihr Sohn?*', but this time stressing the word *Ihr*. Use your pointing finger to demonstrate the difference between *mein* and *Ihr*. If I continue asking learners about their children, they will keep answering *mein*, so I have to ask questions about my family. The family tree is still up on the board showing people's first names, so I just ask '*Wer ist Jane? Wer ist Lizzie? Wer ist Bert?*', etc to elicit the responses '*Das ist Ihr(e)* . . .'

I will have asked my group the previous week to bring in some family photos (I will have stressed close family members to avoid getting involved with too much vocabulary). I make sure that learners can ask '*Wer ist das?*' and '*Ist das Ihr . . ?*' and the class now splits into small groups where they show their photos to the other group members who try and find out who everyone is. Not everyone will have remembered to bring in photographs, but they can still join a group and ask about other people's family.

Inevitably, people will need vocabulary for other family members who are on the photographs. If the earlier part of the lesson went really well and learners picked up the new words quickly, I might have added other words, e.g. aunt, nephew, cousin at that stage. Otherwise I will give the new words to the individual groups as they crop up.

If you want to organise a pair exercise without the use of photos, get each learner to write the names of a few people who are close to them on a bit of paper, give this list to their partner and the couples can ask each other '*Wer ist Jonathan?*', '*Wer ist Zenab?*' or even try guessing '*Ist Edith Ihre Großmutter?*', scoring a point for each correct guess. Learners can also try and build up a family tree for their partner. If you have already covered the accusative case *einen* (and you will have done if you have reached Lesson 2 of *Deutsch Direkt*, for example), learners can try and make up a family tree for their partner by asking questions such as '*Haben Sie einen Großvater?*'

One word of warning — sometimes people do not like talking about their family or lack of family! If you sense that anyone might be sensitive about this, give out role cards of fictitious German-sounding characters for learners to base their answers on.

You will find that a lot of vocabulary has been presented in this lesson. In addition to the suggestions above, words like *verheiratet, getrennt,* etc often come up naturally during discussions. It therefore makes sense to stick to just *mein* and *Ihr* for this lesson.

Next lesson you can introduce *sein, ihr,* etc. In an adult class I do not think it is worth teaching *dein* and *euer* in the early stages, nor, for that matter, the *du* or *ihr* forms of verbs, since the *Sie* form will be far more useful when dealing with Germans. Either take one learner's family tree which was built up in the previous lesson as a model, use your own again, use the royal family (if you can keep up with who is still married to whom) or just make up a model family tree.

Show the diagram below, where each person in the royal family is allocated a number. Start off by quickly revising vocabulary, e.g.:

Teacher: *2 und 5*
Learners: *Vater und Sohn*

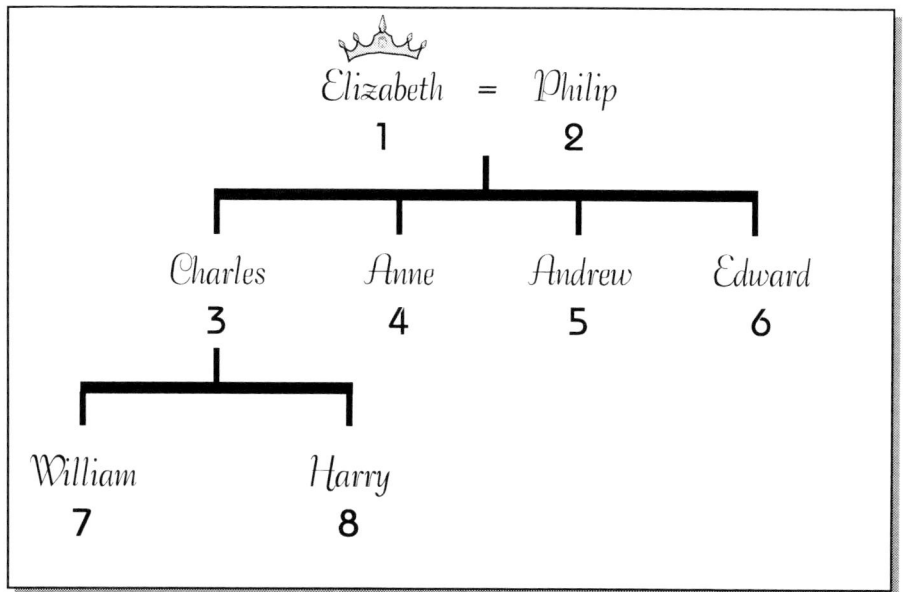

This leads neatly to the point of today's lesson as you say '*Das ist Philip und das ist **sein** Sohn*'. Then tell learners to answer everything from, say, William's point of view, so I ask '*Wer ist Anne, Harry?*', etc to say '*Das ist seine Tante, sein Bruder*'. Go through various male members of the family giving plenty of opportunity for repetition of the new possessive adjective *sein* but also plenty of revision of vocabulary.

I prefer to start off with *sein* as, if I started with *ihr,* learners might confuse it with the *Ihr* they were practising last week. Having had plenty of practice with *sein,* however, learners will be used to talking about a third person and will be in the swing of the exercise. *Unser* can be practised by asking your students to imagine how the Queen and Prince Philip or Princes William and Harry would reply in German to questions such as '*Wer ist Andrew?*'

Since the pattern of endings is the same as *mein* and *Ihr,* as well as for *ein* and *kein*, students do not need such extensive practice of these forms by this stage.

Over to you

Task 1 — Would colour coding be appropriate when presenting possessive adjectives in your language? Think how you could build colour into your presentation.

Task 2 — How might you present possessive adjectives in a business class? Devise a 'tree', but this time, instead of listing family members, write names and job titles to practise 'my boss, her secretary, his colleague, our marketing director', etc.

The use of the genitive case after the negative: 'У МЕНЯ НЕТ' *in Russian*

To express 'I have got . . . ' Russian uses an idiomatic expression based on part of the verb 'to be'. This means that, unlike in other languages, you do not have to worry about putting what you have got into the accusative case — it is still the nominative. However, if you want to say 'I haven't got . . . ', the structure becomes more complicated and the English object has to go into the genitive case in Russian.

First let your students be exposed to the new construction lots of times to give them a chance to work out the rules and reasons for themselves, if possible. Either hide an object behind your back or hold up a flashcard facing towards you so that learners do not know what is depicted. Ask students to guess what you have got and each time they guess wrongly, answer in a full sentence using the new construction:

Student 1:	у вас есть книга?
Teacher:	нет, книги у меня нет.
Student 2:	у вас есть чай?
Teacher:	нет, чая у меня нет.
Student 3:	у вас есть открытка?
Teacher:	нет, открытки у меня нет.
Student 4:	у вас есть паспорт?
Teacher:	нет, паспорта у меня нет.

. . . and so on, until they either guess or you bring the activity to a close by telling them what you've got. The object of the activity is for learners to keep guessing wrongly so that you have the chance to repeat the new construction lots of times; do not, therefore, choose anything too obvious. If, however, they do guess too quickly, just choose another object or picture and try again.

By now there will be several learners looking extremely perplexed and even if they gathered that the ending was changing after the negative, they may well want confirmation of this. Ask learners what they noticed and they will either mention just a change of ending or they will recognise it as the genitive ending. Since this is a fairly complicated and unusual structure it is probably best not to introduce it too early on in a course; learners can easily just respond with the one word answer 'No' to the question 'Have you got . . ?' in the early stages. You can thus remind them that they have seen the endings before and elicit from the group that it is the genitive they are using.

Learners have now heard the construction several times, but that does not mean that they will be able to produce the correct genitive form themselves. Before letting them work more independently in pairs or groups, where you will not be able to monitor all that is being said, you will need to set up a situation where learners will produce the negative form. I usually ask learners to be waiters/waitresses in a very poorly stocked cafe or shop assistants in a poorly stocked shop, and that whatever I ask for they have to say they have not got it (see example 'Awkward waiters' p28). As I am controlling the vocabulary used I will ensure that all genders are covered as well as both hard and soft forms to cover all the possible genitive case endings; I will not include irregularities, needless to say. I will write examples on the board and leave them there later on for learners to refer to. If I am covering this structure in a Level 1 course, I will probably stick to singular forms and not mention adjective endings at all, but this whole activity can be repeated yet made much more challenging at later stages in the course when the genitive plural is introduced, or when you wish to practise or revise adjective endings.

Only when I am sure that learners have assimilated the genitive case endings, do I move on to pair work, although with elementary levels I will probably control the language that is to be used at this stage too. The activity *Contraband* (see *Language games and activities* in the CILT Network series, p.13) is ideal for pairwork. I hand out a list of ten items that students might be trying to smuggle through customs e.g.:

| фотоаппарат |
| пиво |
| водка |
| гашиш |
| наркотики |
| табак |
| сигареты |
| револьвер |
| икона |
| бриллианты |

(camera, beer, vodka, hashish, drugs, tobacco, cigarettes, a revolver, an icon, diamonds)

and ask students to tick on their own list three items that they have decided to 'smuggle'. Their partner has to find out what they have ticked by asking 'у вас есть фотоаппарат?', etc ('Have you got a/any . . ?'), and if their partner has not ticked that item he or she can respond with a full sentence.

If you are happy for learners to use vocabulary that they have thought up themselves (but remember, they will come up with plurals, nouns that are irregular and so on), this structure is ideally suited to a guessing game. Hand out a picture of an object to each learner, with the instruction that they must not show it to their partner. The task is to guess what their partner has got in their hands by guessing 'Have you got a bottle of wine?', etc. Ideally there will be lots of wrong guesses, giving the pairs plenty of opportunity of using the genitive case to express 'у меня нет . . .'.

If you have recently covered a certain topic area with the class, e.g. hotels, fruit and vegetables, bring this new vocabulary into the activity as useful revision by getting learners to imagine they are hotel managers or market stall holders. If you have a large group, you can play a 'shopping' or 'finding a suitable hotel' game. Half the class are hotel managers or stall holders and they write down three or four facilities or types of fruits and vegetables that they 'have'. The other half of the class are customers or guests and write down three facilities they would require in a hotel or three food items on their shopping list. These people have to 'buy' all the items on their list or find a hotel that matches their requirements by going round the hotel managers or stall holders asking 'у вас есть бассейн?' or 'у вас есть яблоки?' (Have you got a swimming pool, apples?).

Over to you

Task If you teach French or German, could you use any of the above activities to introduce and practise *'Je n'ai pas de . . .'* and *kein*? What changes would you make?

Comparative of adjectives in English

By the time that comparatives are introduced, learners will already know lots of different adjectives. Base the context of the presentation on what they already know. The transport context described below is just one of many possibilities. It is better not to use learners in the classroom as examples when using the comparative as some people get embarrassed when the language is too personal, e.g. who is older, bigger, fatter, thinner?

Show the class a picture of a car, preferably a fairly sporty pricey model, although not the top of the range. Elicit a range of adjectives by asking the group 'What can you tell me about this Golf? Is it cheap? Is it fast or slow? Is it comfortable? Is it difficult to park?' As learners give an answer containing an adjective which you intend to put in the comparative form later, write it up on the board. It is important to know what activity you plan to do next, so you know which words are relevant. I plan to compare the Golf with an even faster, more expensive car, so I do not write up words such as 'red, green, German'. If people answer using a phrase such as 'It travels 50 miles to the gallon', I teach or elicit an appropriate adjective, such as 'economical'. The answer 'It uses a lot of petrol' is all right, though, as later, even though 'a lot of' is not an adjective, I can give the form 'more petrol'. After a brainstorming session lasting a few minutes, the board might look like this:

fast	beautiful, attractive
easy to park	economical
it has a big boot	comfortable

Note that I have written the phrases in two columns; the column on the right contains longer words which form their comparative by adding the word 'more'.

Now bring out a second picture, this time a Ferrari, or something similar, and ask various yes/no questions 'Is this car fast/expensive/easy to park?', etc. Now expose the learners to the new construction by asking 'Which is faster, the Golf or the Ferrari? Which is more expensive?' Writing up the prices and top speed of each car, and drawing attention to these figures as you use the comparative form, will let learners know that you are comparing the two things. Continue, using the phrases you have written up on the board. If an irregular adjective like 'good' was elicited earlier, then ensure that learners realise how its comparative is formed by drawing attention to it. Say 'The Golf is a good car, the Ferrari is a good car too, but which is **better,** do you think?' Everyone will realise that 'better' is the comparative of 'good' without your needing to talk about exceptions to the rule, if you say 'fast, faster, expensive, more expensive, good, better'.

To ensure that learners grasp the new form and apply it correctly, continue with some more teacher-controlled oral practice. Show two different pictures of various forms of transport, say a bicycle and a bus, a motor cycle and a train — you can also bring in a bit of humour by showing a donkey, camel or a tractor — and ask 'What can you say about these?' The fact that learners have just been comparing a Golf and a Ferrari means that they will answer your question using comparatives. Throw in other appropriate adjectives from time to time by asking 'Which is healthier/safer/more convenient?', then write these words, too, on the board in the right column, so that learners can use them themselves in later examples.

I like to use the context of transport because it gives scope for practice with lots of different adjectives, but any two things can be compared, depending on your class's interests. Make sure that you choose two things that are sufficiently different for there to be no ambiguity. Asking learners to compare Milton Keynes and Venice will come up with more vocabulary than if you ask them to compare Venice and Florence.

The comparative is not a difficult structure and learners should have had plenty of practice in a whole group situation by now. Tell your class they are going to work in pairs and set up the situation. For a confident group, say that each partner is trying to sell you, the tutor, their car; you only want to buy one car, so they have to make a very good case for their make of car. Give out a picture of a car to each person and say that this is 'their' car. Although it doesn't matter what makes you use, make sure that each pair has two reasonably different types of cars, so that they can actually be compared. Imagine one partner (A) has been given a Fiat Uno and the other a BMW; the conversation might go like this:

A My car is cheaper than your car.
B Yes, but my car is faster than your car. And it's more comfortable for long journeys.
A Yes, but your car is much more expensive; it uses more petrol too.

You will have to go around to each pair and listen to their reasons, or at least to their summing up, so that you can decide which car to 'buy'. Another possibility is to divide the class into threes with the third person playing the role of the buyer. He or she can make up their own mind then as to whose arguments have swayed them the most.

Obviously, in a very free activity like this you do not know what each pair or group will say; it does generate an enormous amount of language, in addition to the comparative, and learners get very involved in the situation. For a more controlled pair work practice using the same pictures tell learners that they each have to say one positive point about their own car or one negative thing about their partner's in turn; they must not repeat adjectives and the game continues until one partner runs out of things to say. You can also do this going round the whole class.

One word of warning — in most languages the comparative will be introduced before possessive pronouns ('mine', 'yours', etc) are known, so make sure that learners do not try to use these forms in the pair practice. This usually means that you should encourage them to repeat the noun (. . . than your car or . . . than the BMW), or just miss it out altogether — my car is more economical.

Over to you

Task 1 If the learners in your group are all from one town, could you build that into your presentation? What would be a good place to compare your town with? Think of at least ten adjectives, e.g. modern, interesting, quiet, that you could practise using this situation.

Task 2 What context could you think up to present the comparative to a class of business people so that you use words like high turnover, profitable and wide range?

Conclusion

Anything can be made boring or interesting, lively or dull, relevant or irrelevant, easy to understand or impossible for even the brainiest person to understand, it is all a matter of presentation. There is a comedian with the catchphrase 'It's the way I tell 'em', meaning that it is not the content of the joke itself that is inherently amusing but the way it is told. This same catchphrase could be applied to teaching the grammar of a language — it is the way grammar is presented and practised in class that motivates learners or switches them right off.

This book has shown that learning grammar can be painless; grammar games can be fun, drills can be amusing, exercises can be interesting and the class can get plenty of oral practice.

Fun and enjoyment are all very well, but we should bear in mind the purpose of teaching grammar. Learners' most important objective is to be able to communicate in the target language. When it comes to deciding what and how to teach, we should remember this ultimate aim and ensure that our methods will enable learners to take one more step towards this goal.

Grammar is only a means to an end. The end is to be able to **use** the language. Grammar is a tool to enable us to do this. It is just as much an inherent part of the language as are pronunciation, intonation, register and vocabulary. Getting any of these essential elements wrong may prevent us from using the language in the way we intended.

By teaching learners grammatical rules, we are giving them power, independence and the confidence to know that by looking up unknown vocabulary they can slot it into a pattern that holds good for any context. By the time they have covered all the cases, tenses, etc there is literally **nothing** they cannot say.

Without grammar language is just a list of disjointed words strung together. Grammar is the skeleton that holds the language together and gives it its form and meaning. Let us not keep the skeleton hidden in the closet, let us bring it out into the open and give it its due status in language learning.

Further reading

Aitken R, *Teaching tenses* (Thomas Nelson and Sons, 1992)

Halliwell S, Pathfinder 17: *Grammar matters* (CILT, 1993)

Harmer J, *Teaching and learning grammar* (Longman, 1987)

King L and P Boaks (eds), *Grammar! A conference report* (CILT, 1994)

Langran J and S Purcell, *Language games and activities* (CILT 1994)

Rinvolucri M, *Grammar games* (Cambridge University Press, 1984; reprinted 1992)

Taylor A, *Teaching and learning grammar* (ALL/ Mary Glasgow Publications, 1994)

Ur P, *Grammar practice activities* (Cambridge University Press, 1988)

Resources

Miniflashcard language games (various languages). See in particular 'Fun with functions' and 'Groovy grammar games'. Available from Miniflashcard Language Games, PO Box 1526, London W7 1ND.